Superfood Rec[...] Delightful Spice: Sumac!

Learn How To Create Versatile Worthy Meals Using Delicious & Powerful Anti-Inflammatory Sumac!

Version 2.0

2021 Edition

Copyright©The-Timeless-Collection-Ltd-2021

Contents

About the Delightful Spice, Sumac

A History

Sumac Rhus Coriaria is a beloved spice in the Middle Eastern and Mediterranean kitchen, used in meat spice rubs to drinks and everything in between. The delightfully vibrant, red cones are ground down into a coarse powder and have a lemony, tangy flavor. Due to its poison berry cousin, sumac is largely misunderstood but the edible sumac boasts so many incredible health benefits that it has become our mission to bring this delightful spice to your kitchen!

Health Benefits

Sumac scores very highly* on the ORAC (Oxygen Radical Absorbance Capacity) Chart, which tests the total antioxidant capacity of a food. Sumac places higher than turmeric, blueberries and acai powder! Due to its antioxidant and anti-inflammatory* properties, this suggests that sumac is highly effective at protecting vulnerable molecules from free radical damage (damage to cells, proteins and DNA).

Interesting Notes

In Ayurvedic teachings, there are six tastes* that have an essential role in our overall health and wellbeing. There are some tastes that are easily recognizable such as sweet, sour and salty but the astringent taste which cleanses your mouth is not very well-known Sumac has this illusive astringent taste and so equipping yourself with this book of recipes means that you're ahead of the health game.

We hope you enjoy the following delicious recipes all starring the incredible, **superfood spice, sumac!**

Sources

USDA Database for the Oxygen Radical Absorbance Capacity (ORAC) of Selected Foods, Release 2 - Prepared by Nutrient Data Laboratory, Beltsville Human Nutrition Research Center (BHNRC), Agricultural Research Service (ARS), U.S. Department of Agriculture (USDA) - May 2010

Antioxidant and anti-inflammatory activities of pyranoanthocyanins and other polyphenols from stag horn sumac (Rhus hirta L.) in Caco-2 cell models - You Peng, Hua Zhang, Ronghua Liu, Yoshinori Minec, Jason McCallum, Chris Kirby, Rong Tsao - Journey of Functional Foods - Volume 20 - Pgs. 139-147 - January 2016

Exploring Ayurvedic Knowledge on Food and Health for Providing Innovative Solutions to Contemporary Healthcare - Unnikrishnan Payyappallimana and Padma Venkatasubramanian - Frontiers in Public Health - March 2016

Disclaimer

None of the information or health statements made here should be taken as a substitute for advice from your doctor or other qualified clinician.

Breakfasts

- Glazed Baked Peaches with Mascarpone & Pumpkin Seeds

- Eggs Royale with a Sumac Hollandaise

- Orange Cardamom Pancakes with Sumac Syrup

- Spiced Tofu Scramble with Cherry Tomatoes

Glazed Baked Peaches with Mascarpone & Pumpkin Seeds

Bake up a larger batch of these delightful peaches and enjoy them in an afternoon pick-me-up yogurt parfait!

Ingredients

- 4 Peaches
- 4 tbsp. Pumpkin Seeds
- 2 tbsp. Pine Honey
- 4 tbsp. Mascarpone

- A few sprigs of Fresh Thyme
- 1 tbsp. Butter
- 2 tbsp. Sumac

Nutrition Values

- 222 kcal per serving
- Total Fat: 14.2g
- Saturated Fat: 6.2g
- Net Carbohydrates: 21.2g
- Sugar: 18.4g

- Fiber: 2.9g
- Protein: 5.4g
- Sodium: 28.9mg
- Cholesterol: 27.8mg

 Cook time
30 minutes

 Prep. time
5 minutes

 Servings
2

Cooking Steps

1. Preheat the oven to 374 F.

2. Slice the peaches in half and de-seed them.

3. Place them in a heavy-based baking tray.

4. In a saucepan, put the honey, thyme leaves, butter and sumac on a low heat.

5. Allow for the honey to melt and bubble a little for 2 minutes, before turning off the heat.

6. Using a pastry brush, spread the honey mixture over the flesh of the peaches in a thick coat. You'll have a little honey left in the pan, set aside.

7. Put them in the oven for 20 minutes.

8. After, take them out and brush them with the remaining honey and put them back in the oven for a further 10 minutes.

9. Place two peaches on each plate and serve them warm with a spoon of mascarpone, or even yogurt, and a sprinkle of pumpkin seeds.

Eggs Royale with Sumac Hollandaise

Create this delicious breakfast for a Sunday brunch, holiday or special occasion. The buttery rich hollandaise pairs perfectly with the fresh salmon and crunchy green asparagus.

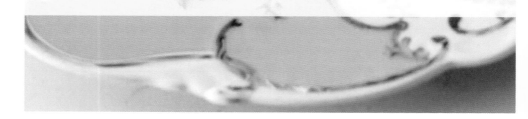

Ingredients

- 7.05oz. (199.8 g) Unsalted Butter
- 4 Large Egg Yolks
- Juice of Half a Lemon
- 2 tsps. of Sumac Water
- 1 tbsp. Extra-Virgin Olive Oil
  Handful of Baby Spinach
- 4 Large Eggs

- 14 oz.(396 g) Fine Asparagus, tailed
- 2 tbsps. Vinegar
- 7oz. (199 g) Sustainably Sourced Smoked Salmon
- 2 Sesame Bagels or English muffins sliced in half and toasted.

Nutrition Values

- 780 kcal per serving
- Total Fat: 59.8g
- Saturated Fat: 31.5g
- Net Carbohydrates: 32.8g
- Sugar: 7.1g

- Fiber: 3.1g
- Protein: 27.6g
- Sodium: 976.1mg
- Cholesterol: 370mg

 Cook time
5 minutes

 Prep. time
30 minutes

 Servings
2

Cooking Steps

1. First, make the hollandaise. Gently melt the butter in a small pan and set aside.

2. Put a large saucepan on filled over halfway with water and two tablespoons of vinegar. Cover with a lid and allow it to come to the boil for your eggs later.

3. In a heatproof bowl, which fits over a small saucepan, whisk together the egg yolks and keep half an eggshell to measure out the water.

4. Set the bowl over a shallow amount of simmering water in a saucepan.

5. Whisk the egg yolks until they form a mayonnaise consistency and then take the pan off the heat. Keep the bowl over the warm water but place a kitchen towel underneath the bowl.

6. In a slow stream, pour all the melted butter into the egg whilst whisky vigorously. Stop halfway through and whisk in the lemon juice to loosen to sauce.

7. Season the sauce with sumac, a pinch of sea salt and sprinkle of pepper. Taste to adjust the seasoning.

8. Pour the hollandaise into a thermos flask while you cook the rest of your breakfast to keep it in a warm condition.

9. Next, blanch your prepared asparagus. Dunk the asparagus into your egg pan of boiling water and let them cook for 2-3 minutes. Take them out using tongs and set them on some kitchen paper to dry.

10. Cut your bagels or muffins in half and lightly toast and butter them. Top them with the spinach, smoked salmon and asparagus.

11. Now, poach the eggs. Turn the heat back up on your egg pan and using a spoon, swirl the water into a whirlpool motion.

12. Crack two of your four eggs into the moving water at either end of the pan. You can use a wooden spoon to push any stray egg whites over the egg.

13. Put a timer on for 3-4 minutes, depending on how cooked you like your eggs.

14. Remove them using a slotted spoon and place them on a clean kitchen towel to absorb any excess water. Cook your next two eggs the same.

15. Plate the eggs on top of the prepared muffin and pour over your hollandaise sauce equally over the four plates.

16. Serve with an extra sprinkle of sumac or a few chopped chives and some sea salt.

Orange Cardamom Pancakes with Sumac Syrup

This citrus, sweet syrup will keep for up to a week in the fridge. Drizzle over granola, fruit bowls and other sweet treats to add a delicate sweet essence.

Ingredients

- 1 tsp. Baking Powder
- 6.35oz. (180 g) Plain Flour
- 1 tsp. Bicarbonate of Soda
- Pinch of Table Salt
- 1 Large Egg
- 1 cup Oat Milk
- 2 tbsp. Coconut Oil, melted

- 1 tbsp. Cinnamon Sugar
- Zest of 1 Orange
- 1 drop of Cardamom essence
- 1 cup of Caster Sugar
- 1 cup of Water
- 1 tsp. of Rosewater Essence
- 2 tbsp. of Sumac

Nutrition Values

- 343 kcal per serving
- Total Fat: 6.2g
- Saturated Fat: 3.7g
- Net Carbohydrates: 64.9g
- Sugar: 35.4g

- Fiber: 1.5g
- Protein: 6.5g
- Sodium: 46mg
- Cholesterol: 46.5mg

 Cook time
20 minutes

 Prep. time
30 minutes

 Servings
4

Cooking Steps

1. Preheat Preheat oven to 122 F.

2. Mix together the flour, baking powder, bicarbonate of soda, salt and cinnamon sugar in a large bowl.

3. Make a well in the center and crack in the egg, pour in the milk and half of the coconut oil. Whisk with an electric hand-held whisk until smooth.

4. Allow the mixture to stand for 30 minutes.

5. Meanwhile, make the syrup by heating 1 cup of water and 1 cup of sugar in a non-stick saucepan over a medium heat.

6. Allow the sugar to melt and gently stir it into the water. Bring the mixture to a boil, then reduce the heat and let it bubble for 5-7 minutes.

7. Add the rosewater and the sumac and allow the syrup to infuse and cool.

8. Heat a pancake pan on a medium-low heat with the remaining coconut oil.

9. Take a serving spoon of mix, per pancake, and dollop onto the pan, spreading into a circular shape. You can probably fit about three on the pan at once.

10. Cook the pancakes for 2 minutes on one side, or until the batter has bubbles in it or the flip side is golden brown.

11. Flip the pancake over and cook for 1 minute. Stack your pancakes on a tray in the slightly heated oven to keep them warm.

12. Repeat this process until you are out of batter.

13. Stack the pancakes on a plate and drizzle over the sumac syrup. Serve with fresh berries and yogurt or mascarpone.

Spiced Tofu Scramble with Cherry Tomatoes

Once you've got the base tofu recipe down, you can add more veggies to the skillet! We love wilted spinach, mushrooms, asparagus or your favorite vegan cheeses!

Ingredients

- 16oz. (453g) Firm or Silken Tofu
- 1 Garlic Clove, minced
- 3 Scallions
- 1 tsp. Ground Turmeric
- 1 tbsp. Ground Sumac
- 1 tsp. Ground Coriander
- 1 cup of Cherry Tomatoes, quartered
- Pinch of Sea Salt
- Drizzle of Olive Oil
- 1 tbsp. Onion Granules

Nutrition Values

- 154 kcal per serving
- Total Fat: 10.8g
- Saturated Fat: 3.3g
- Net Carbohydrates: 5g
- Sugar: 1.5g
- Fiber: 0.6g
- Protein: 11.5g
- Sodium: 209.2mg
- Cholesterol: 10mg

 Cook time
5 minutes

 Prep. time
5 minutes

 Servings
4

Cooking Steps

1. Into a bowl, crumble the tofu, add the garlic, onions, spices, onion granules and sea salt. Mix and set aside.

2. In a skillet, heat a tbsp of olive oil on a medium heat.

3. Add the tofu mixture and cook for 5 minutes.

4. Add the cherry tomatoes and feta cheese and cook for another 5 minutes.

5. Serve the scrambled tofu on your choice of toast, with a drizzle of olive oil, spring onions and herbs.

Main Dishes

- Sumac Vegetable Risotto With Grilled Asparagus

- Sirloin Steak With Sumac Mint Chimichurri

- Pistachio Sumac Crusted Haddock Fillets

- Wild Mushroom Zaatar Puff Pie

- Sticky Sumac & Orange Glazed Chicken Thighs

Sumac Vegetable Risotto with Grilled Asparagus

One of our summer's day favorites, this grilled vegetable risotto is wholesome but light for a chill afternoon or date night. Sprinkle over some nutritional yeast instead of parmesan for nuttiness.

Ingredients

- 1 Carrot, small-diced
- 1 cup of Peas
- 8.8oz. (249g) of Asparagus
- 1 tbsp. of Tomato Paste
- 2 Low-Sodium Vegetable Stock Cubes
- 2 ⅓ cups of White Wine
- 3 Garlic Cloves, minced
- 3 Sprigs of Mint, chopped
- A bunch of Parsley, chopped
- A handful of Basil, chopped
- 1 Shallot, minced
- 6 ½ cups of Boiling Water
- 1 tbsp. Olive Oil
- 1 tbsp. Extra-Virgin Olive Oil
- 1 tbsp. Sumac
- 2 cups Arborio Rice
- 1 cup of Nutritional Yeast

Nutrition Values

- 437 kcal per serving
- Total Fat: 13.3g
- Saturated Fat: 2.3g
- Net Carbohydrates: 42.3g
- Sugar: 7.2g
- Fiber: 5.6g
- Protein: 14.6g
- Sodium: 685.1mg
- Cholesterol: 7.5mg

 Cook time
40 minutes

 Prep. time
15 minutes

 Servings
4

Cooking Steps

1. Make the vegetable stock using the two cubes and the water.
2. In a large deep-sided pan, heat the olive oil and butter in a pan on medium.
3. Add the shallots and carrots and sweat until softened.
4. Add the garlic, tomato paste and the rice and fry for about 3 minutes.
5. Pour over the white wine and allow for the rice to absorb it. Season with liberally with pepper, sumac and the parsley.
6. Add a ladle full of stock and stir. Let the rice absorb the stock, then add another ladle full. Repeat this until all the stock is absorbed.

7. Stir through the risotto, the peas, mint and basil and turn the heat to low and top with a lid.

8. Meanwhile, turn the grill or broiler on high, rub the asparagus in olive oil and sea salt and place under the grill. Allow them to cook for 10 minutes.

9. Taste the risotto and season will the salt as required.

10. Serve in pasta dishes, with the asparagus placed on top and a sprinkle of sumac.

Sirloin Steak with Sumac Mint Chimichurri

We love the tanginess the sumac adds to the chimichurri in this meal. Add a side dish of sautéed greens and you've got a show stopping Friday night dinner!

Ingredients

- 1 Carrot, small-diced
- 1 cup of Peas
- 8.8oz. (249g) of Asparagus
- 1 tbsp. of Tomato Paste
- 2 Low-Sodium Vegetable Stock Cubes
- 2 ⅓ cups of White Wine
- 3 Garlic Cloves, minced
- 3 Sprigs of Mint, chopped
- A bunch of Parsley, chopped
- A handful of Basil, chopped
- 1 Shallot, minced
- 6 ½ cups of Boiling Water
- 1 tbsp. Olive Oil
- 1 tbsp. Extra-Virgin Olive Oil
- 1 tbsp. Sumac
- 2 cups Arborio Rice
- 1 cup of Nutritional Yeast

Nutrition Values

- 579 kcal per serving
- Total Fat: 45.2g
- Saturated Fat: 1.5g
- Net Carbohydrates: 8.3g
- Sugar: 2g
- Fiber: 0.8g
- Protein: 31.6g
- Sodium: 60mg
- Cholesterol: 74mg

 Cook time
20 minutes

 Prep. time
2.5 hours

 Servings
4

Cooking Steps

1. Make chimichurri by finely dicing the shallot and red chilli, and finely chopping the mint, oregano, parsley and cilantro.

2. In a bowl, mix the garlic, shallot, red chilli, chopped herbs, lemon juice and white wine vinegar.

3. Add the olive oil, vermouth and sumac. Season to taste.

4. Pour half the chimichurri over the steaks and massage the sauce into the meat. Put in the fridge for two hours along with the other bowl of chimichurri.

5. An hour before cooking, take out the steak and let it come to room temperature before cooking.

6. Preheat the oven to 356 F.

7. Heat a large pan on high heat until smoking hot.

8. Cook for 1-2 minutes on either side and then put on a tray in the oven for 5 minutes.

9. Take out the steak and let them rest for 10 minutes.

10. Slice the steak on a wooden board and then drizzle with the chimichurri sauce.

Pistachio Sumac Crusted Haddock Fillets

Whip up some of these delicious fillets to store in the freezer and enjoy them over salads, a bed of pasta or next to some healthy greens! Sub out the extra virgin olive oil for coconut or even avocado oil.

Ingredients

- 1 cup of shelled unsalted Pistachios
- 1 cup of Breadcrumbs
- 1 cup of Ground Almonds
- 4 fillets of Haddock, skinned
- 1 cup of Parsley

- 2tbsp of Sumac
- 1tbsp Sea Salt
- 1tbsp of Pepper
- 1 Egg Yolk
- Extra Virgin Olive Oil
- Juice of Half of Lemon

Nutrition Values

- 412 kcal per serving
- Total Fat: 30.3g
- Saturated Fat: 3.4g
- Net Carbohydrates: 24.6g
- Sugar: 4.3g

- Fiber: 6.3g
- Protein: 33g
- Sodium: 157.1mg
- Cholesterol: 46mg

 Cook time
13 minutes

 Prep. time
20 minutes

 Servings
4

Cooking Steps

1. Preheat oven to 392 F.
2. In a food processor, blend together the pistachios, breadcrumbs, ground almonds, lemon, parsley, sea salt, pepper, egg yolk and olive oil.
3. If the crust mixture is too dry, add some extra olive oil.
4. Mix in a bowl the lemon and olive oil and using a pastry brush, coat the fish fillets with the liquid.
5. Place the fish fillets onto a baking tray lined with parchment paper.
6. Spoon and pat the crust on top of the fillets, until all the mixture is used up. It doesn't matter how thick the crust is, pat it down to compact it onto the fillet.
7. Bake the fish in the oven for 13 minutes. Be careful not to over-bake the fish, you want it to flake and be shiny but not translucent. .

Wild Mushroom Zaatar Puff Pie

All the unique flavors of the Middle-East, through thyme and sumac and all the comfort of a delicious, hot pie!

Ingredients

- 10.6oz. (300.50g) dried Porcini mushrooms, chopped
- 1 lb.(453 g) Chestnut Mushrooms
- 0.5 lb.(226 g) Wild Mushrooms
- 7oz. (198g) Cavolo Nero
- 5 Garlic Cloves, minced
- 2 sprigs of fresh Thyme
- 1 tbsp. of dried Tarragon
- 1 tbsp. of Sumac
- 0.4 cups of Vermouth

- 2 tbsp. of Olive Oil
- 1 Shallot, diced
- 2 Bay Leaves
- 1 tbsp. of Soy Sauce
- 1 handful of Parsley, chopped
- 4.2 cups of Vegetable Stock
- 2 tbsp. Vegan Butter
- Salt & Black Pepper
- Roll of Puff Pastry

Nutrition Values

- 305 kcal per serving
- Total Fat: 15.1g
- Saturated Fat: 5.5g
- Net Carbohydrates: 22.5g
- Sugar: 2.6g

- Fiber: 18.3g
- Protein: 14.2g
- Sodium: 317.7mg
- Cholesterol: 10mg

 Cook time
40 minutes

 Prep. time
60 minutes

 Servings
6

Cooking Steps

1. Heat the stock over a medium heat. Steep the dried porcini mushrooms in the hot stock and set aside.

2. In a casserole pan, melt 1tbsp of butter over a medium heat and fry the onions until they are softened and caramelised.

3. Ensuring the mushrooms are clean, chop the big ones into quarters and the smaller into halves, depending on size.

4. Sauté the wild mushrooms with half the garlic over a medium heat until they begin to soften (2-3 minutes). Add half the vermouth, cook for another minute and tip into a bowl and set aside.

5. Pour in the stock, then add the rest of the mushrooms, the bay leaves, the cavolo nero, herbs and the seasonings.

6. Boil for 10 minutes, tip into the pie dish and allow to cool completely.

7. Preheat the oven to 356 F.

8. Roll out the pastry to a thickness of about 3mm. Cut a long strip off the pastry, just wider than the rim of the pie dish. Wet the rim with a little water, then press the pastry strip down onto it. Brush the strip with a little more water, then lay the sheet of rolled-out pastry on top. Press down firmly along the edges to seal, then trim off any excess.

9. Cut a few slits in the pastry topping and glaze by brushing with beaten egg. Bake in the preheated oven for 40 minutes, until the pastry is golden brown and puffed up. Serve immediately.

Sticky Sumac & Orange Glazed Chicken Thighs

We use chicken thighs in this recipe as they are juicier and more flavorsome than chicken breasts! Marinating them in yogurt gives the chicken even more tenderness.

Ingredients

- 4 tbsp. Greek Yogurt
- 1.5lbs Boneless, Skinless, Chicken Thighs
- 1 tbsp. Sesame Oil
- 2 Garlic Cloves, minced
- 3 tbsp. Runny Honey
- 2 tbsp. Sumac
- Sea Salt
- Juice of Half a Lemon

Nutrition Values

- 233 kcal per serving
- Total Fat: 9.4g
- Saturated Fat: 2g
- Net Carbohydrates: 8.6g
- Sugar: 8.3g
- Fiber: 0.3g
- Protein: 30.7g
- Sodium: 375mg
- Cholesterol: 128.3mg

 Cook time
20 minutes

 Prep. time
6 hours

 Servings
4

Cooking Steps

1. Put the skinless chicken thighs in a bowl with the Greek yogurt, lemon juice, sesame oil and garlic.

2. Cover and put in the fridge overnight or during the day.

3. Take the chicken out of the fridge for an hour to let the chicken come to temperature.

4. Heat the grill or broiler on high.

5. Shake the yogurt marinade mostly off the thighs and brush them with the honey. Make sure they are well coated on all sides.

6. Put them under the grill for about 6 minutes on each side.

7. Take them out and heat a pan with a thin layer of olive on high.

8. Add the thighs to the pan, giving them 1-2 minutes on each side, letting the remaining honey glaze to caramelize and brown.

9. Serve with a squeeze or lemon and pinch of sea salt.

Side Dishes

- Chickpea Fattoush Salad

- Tenderstem Broccoli With Toasted Almonds And Saffron Yogurt

- Sumac Roasted Potatoes

- Persian Tahdig

Chickpea Fattoush Salad

Opt for fresh herbs to give your Fattoush salad it's famous kick! We served our salad alongside the sweet sticky sumac glazed chicken thighs, for a filling and colorful meal.

Ingredients

- 2 tbsp. Extra Virgin Olive Oil
- 2 Whole Wheat Pitta breads
- A large pinch of Sea Salt
- 2 tbsp. Sumac
- Juice of Half an Orange
- Juice of Half a Lemon
- 1 Garlic Clove, minced
- 2 tbsps. Extra Virgin Olive Oil
- 14oz. (397g) Cherry Tomatoes, halved

- 1 Cucumber, chopped
- 1 Red Onion, diced
- 2 heads Romaine Lettuce, shredded
- Handful of Parsley leaves, chopped
- Handful of Mint leaves, chopped
- 2 cups of Cooked Chickpeas
- 5 tbsps. Greek Yogurt
- Sprinkle of Cumin
- 2 tbsps. of Tahini Paste
- Salt & Pepper

Nutrition Values

- 493 kcal per serving
- Total Fat: 24g
- Saturated Fat: 4g
- Net Carbohydrates: 55.5g
- Sugar: 15.7g

- Fiber: 12.3g
- Protein: 16.2g
- Sodium: 122.4mg
- Cholesterol: 0mg

 Cook time
10 minutes

 Prep. time
10 minutes

 Servings
4

Cooking Steps

1. Open out the pitta into halves and tear them up into bite size pieces. Brush them with olive oil, flaky sea salt and sumac.

2. Toast under the grill until they're nice and crisp.

3. Mix the salad ingredients together; the tomatoes, cucumber, red onion and lettuce.

4. Make the salad dressing by whisking together the orange juice, lemon juice, garlic, fresh herbs and olive oil.

5. In the oven, at 392 F, bake the chickpeas until they are slightly dried/ browned.

6. For the topping, mix the yogurt with the cumin and the tahini paste and season with salt and pepper, to taste

7. Using a deep platter, layer the salad and then the pitta breads on top. Spoon the yogurt on top and sprinkle with sumac, chickpeas, pomegranate seeds and any leftover fresh herbs.

8. Make the salad dressing by whisking together the orange juice, lemon juice, garlic, fresh herbs and olive oil.

9. In the oven, at 392 F, bake the chickpeas until they are slightly dried/ browned.

10. For the topping, mix the yogurt with the cumin and the tahini paste and season with salt and pepper, to taste.

11. Using a deep platter, layer the salad and then the pitta breads on top. Spoon the yogurt on top and sprinkle with sumac, chickpeas, pomegranate seeds and any leftover fresh herbs.

.

Tenderstem Broccoli with Toasted Almonds and Saffron Yogurt

The flaked almonds taste creamy and delicious paired with the saffron yogurt and crunchy broccoli. You can swap out other vegetables here, such as asparagus, Brussels *sprouts or long beans!*

Ingredients

- 7oz. (198.4g) Broccolini / Tenderstem Broccoli
- 1oz. (28.3g) Flaked Almonds
- 1 tsp. Lemon Juice
- 1 tsp. Salt

- ½ tsp. Saffron Threads
- 2 tbsp. Boiling Water
- 4 tbsp. Yogurt
- 1 tbsp. Sumac

Nutrition Values

- 69kcal per serving
- Total Fat: 3.8g
- Saturated Fat: 0.3g
- Net Carbohydrates: 4.1g
- Sugar: 1.7g

- Fiber: 0.5g
- Protein: 4.2g
- Sodium: 23.7mg
- Cholesterol: 0mg

 Cook time
10 minutes

 Prep. time
5 minutes

 Servings
4

Cooking Steps

1. Steep the saffron threads in the boiling water and set aside.

2. Heat a pan with filled ¼ with water and bring to simmer.

3. Add the broccoli and put the lid on. Steam for 6-8 minutes.

4. Meanwhile, in a bowl mix the yogurt, saffron water, lemon juice and salt and set aside.

5. Heat a small, dry frying pan on a medium heat. Add the flaked almonds and shake the pan, ensuring they are evenly spread out on the surface.

6. Toss the almonds a few times over a couple of minutes until they catch the heat and brown. They will burn very quickly once lightly browned, so keep an eye out.

7. Drain the broccoli, rinse in cold water, dry and put on a side plate.

8. Top the broccoli with the saffron yogurt, a generous sprinkle of sumac and the toasted almonds.

Sumac Roasted Potatoes

Sumac keeps its entire bright, unique flavor here as it doesn't get heated, giving an extra layer of flavor to these crispy skinned roasters. Save any extras for breakfast frittatas the following day!

Ingredients

- 2 lbs. Russet Potatoes
- ½ cup of Rapeseed Oil or Vegetable Oil
- 1 tbsp. of Malden Salt
- 2 tbsp. Sumac

Nutrition Values

- 544 kcal per serving
- Total Fat: 24.4g
- Saturated Fat: 0g
- Net Carbohydrates: 76.7g
- Sugar: 2.9g
- Fiber: 5.9g
- Protein: 8.8g
- Sodium: 0mg
- Cholesterol: 0mg

 Cook time
60 minutes

 Prep. time
45 minutes

Servings
4-6

Cooking Steps

1. Peel the potatoes and quarter them.
2. Place in a large pan of water and heat to a boil on a high heat.
3. Reduce to a medium heat and cook the potatoes for 10-15 minutes.
4. Preheat the oven to 392 F.
5. Drain the potatoes and put them back in the hot pan to dry out for five minutes.
6. Place on a roasting tray with the oil and salt. Toss the potatoes to ensure they are fully coated.
7. Put the potatoes in the oven and cook for 30-40 minutes, turning halfway through the time.
8. Whilst the potatoes are still hot out the oven, toss them in the sumac and serve with an extra pinch of salt.

Persian Tahdig

This gorgeous, bejeweled platter of rice is a showstopper at any dinner party! Turn this side dish into a main by adding some sautéed, garlic shrimp or Smokey, baked eggplant.

Ingredients

- 3 cups Basmati Rice
- ½ tsp Saffron
- 1 tsp Salt
- 8 cups of Boiling Water
- 2 tbsp Salted Butter
- 3 tbsp Greek Yogurt

- Pomegranate Seeds
- 2 tbsp Sumac
- 2 tbsp Rapeseed Oil
- 1 cup of Pistachios, chopped
- ¼ cup of Water
- 2tbsp Olive Oil

Nutrition Values

- 433 kcal per serving
- Total Fat: 27.8g
- Saturated Fat: 6.3g
- Net Carbohydrates: 53.7g
- Sugar: 2.6g

- Fiber: 3.7g
- Protein: 8.1g
- Sodium: 108mg
- Cholesterol: 12mg

 Cook time
60 minutes

 Prep. time
45 minutes

 Servings
4-6

Cooking Steps

1. Measure your rice out into a large bowl and cover with cold water. Give it a mix and allow it to soak for 45 minutes. Drain with a mesh sieve and heat 8 cups of water in a large pan, with square and deep sides.

2. When the water is boiling, add the drained rice and cook for 6 minutes or until it's al dente.

3. Use some of the boiling water to steep the saffron. Add the threads to 3 tbsp. of boiling water and allow infusing.

4. Drain the rice again immediately and run it under cold water to stop the cooking.

5. Take a heaped cupful of the rice and add it to a bowl with the Greek Yogurt and mix it together.

6. Using the same pot, add the vegetable oil, the butter and half of the saffron liquid. Stir until it has melted and is coating the bottom of the pan.

7. Add the cup of yogurt rice in a layer in the pan. Add the remaining rice on top of this layer, building a pyramid shape away from the edges of the pot. Using a wooden spoon handle, pole six holes carefully in the mound. One hole in the middle and five around it. This will let out the steam out later on.

8. Return to a medium heat and cook until the rice begins to steam. Then add the olive oil, ¼ cup of water and remaining saffron over the rice. The rice around the edges should be bubbling. If not, add a drizzle of oil all around the sides of the pan.

9. Wrap a lid with a kitchen tea-towel and cover the pot. Cook the rice on a medium-low heat for 30 minutes or until crispy and golden.

10. Check if the Tahdig is ready by using an offset knife to gently poke around the edges as we will be flipping the rice onto a plate from the pan.

11. When the Tahdig is ready, turn off the heat, cover the pan with a flat plate and use oven-mitts to pick up the pan and carefully flip the rice on to the plate. Alternatively, use a big spoon to remove the soft rice on to a plate and then use an offset knife to gently peel off the crust and assemble on top of the fluffy rice.

12. Serve with a sprinkle of pomegranates, pistachios and sumac on top.

Dips & Dressings

- Baba Ghanoush

- Spiced Hummus

- Simple Avocado Dip With Sumac

- Greek Yogurt Dip

- Greek Salad Dressing

Baba Ghanoush

Baba Ganoush, characteristically made from eggplants and sesame, is best served chunky alongside some freshly stone-baked bread. Try a fresh baguette, pitta bread or grissini.

Ingredients

- 3 Eggplants, seek out smaller varieties of eggplants which contain less water!
- 1 tbsp Tahini
- 1 tsp Sumac
- Juice of a Lemon
- Handful of Pine-nuts
- 2 cloves of Garlic, minced
- ½ tsp Cumin
- Olive oil
- Sea salt & Pepper

Nutrition Values

- 81 kcal per serving
- Total Fat: 6.4g
- Saturated Fat: 0.9g
- Net Carbohydrates: 5.1g
- Sugar: 2.6g
- Fiber: 2.6g
- Protein: 1.9g
- Sodium: 1.6mg
- Cholesterol: 0mg

 Cook time
45 minutes

 Prep. time
10 minutes

 Servings
4

Cooking Steps

1. Preheat the oven to 356 F.

2. Drizzle the whole eggplants with olive oil and a generous pinch of sea salt. Put them in the oven for 45 minutes.

3. Take them out the oven and, one at a time, put the eggplant in a plastic zip lock bag. Hold the eggplant from its stem at the top with a tea-towel and with your other hand squeeze the eggplant until the flesh falls out of it. It should be easily pulled out. Transfer the flesh to a bowl and repeat this for each eggplant.

4. In a food processor, blitz together the tahini, sumac, lemon, pine-nuts, garlic and cumin with a drizzle of olive oil. Blend until smooth.

5. Add the eggplant flesh and blitz 2-3 times. You don't want the dip to be completely smooth; keeping it chunky will keep the eggplant flavor.

Spiced Hummus

The lemony sumac atop this tasty hummus makes the dish super moreish, so keep extra in a little serving dish to freshen up the hummus as you and your guests go!

Ingredients

- 14 oz. (396.8g). Chickpeas
- ⅓ cup Olive Oil
- ⅕ cup Vegetable Oil
- Juice of 1 Lemon

- 2 Garlic Cloves
- 1 tsp. Paprika
- 2 tsp. Sumac
- ⅓ cup Tahini Paste

Nutrition Values

- 568 kcal per serving
- Total Fat: 44.8g
- Saturated Fat: 6.4g
- Net Carbohydrates: 26.3g
- Sugar: 0.5g

- Fiber: 7.8
- Protein: 17.3g
- Sodium: 320mg
- Cholesterol: 0mg

 Cook time
5 minutes

 Prep. time
10 minutes

 Servings
4

Cooking Steps

1. Warm your olive oil and vegetable oil in a pan over a medium heat.

2. Add half of your oil mixture into the blender, followed by the chickpeas.

3. Begin to blend the mixture, pouring in the remaining oil mixture in slowly.

4. Add your lemon juice, garlic, paprika, sumac and tahini and continue to blend until the hummus is of a smooth consistency.

5. You can add a few tablespoons of water if the hummus is really too thick but persevere with the blender. Keep mixing in between blending to help the hummus move.

6. At the end sprinkle in a tablespoon of salt, mix and taste. Adjust the seasoning. Serve this with warm buttered pitta bread.

Simple Avocado Dip with Sumac

Creamy and delicious, this simple avocado dip goes perfectly with salads, dipped on pita breads or nacho chips, or alongside breakfast eggs.

Ingredients

- 3-4 ripe Avocados
- 1 Garlic Clove, minced
- Juice of 1 Lime
- 1tbsp Lemon Juice

- 1tbsp Sumac
- 1tbsp Sea Salt
- 1tbsp Extra-Virgin Olive Oil

Nutrition Values

- 271 kcal per serving
- Total Fat: 27.5g
- Saturated Fat: 3.5g
- Net Carbohydrates: 4.2g
- Sugar: 0g

- Fiber: 3g
- Protein: 4g
- Sodium: 0.1mg
- Cholesterol: 0mg

 Cook time
5 minutes

 Prep. time
10 minutes

 Servings
4

Cooking Steps

1. Cut the avocados in half and de-stone them. Scoop out the flesh straight into a food processor.

2. In the food processor add the garlic, lemon, lime, sumac, salt and extra virgin olive oil.

3. Blitz until completely blended and silky smooth.

4. Serve with extra sumac sprinkled over.

Greek Yogurt Dip

This cooling, refreshing dip pairs beautifully with freshly cut crudités (or on the side of a BBQ plate). Prepare some veggies at the start of the week and enjoy this dip as an afternoon snack!

Ingredients

- ¾ cup of Greek Yogurt
- Juice of half a Lemon
- 1tbsp Tahini
- 1 Garlic Cloves
- 2 Scallions

- A few sprigs of Parsley
- A few sprigs of Basil
- A few sprigs of Mint
- Salt and Black Pepper

Nutrition Values

- 154 kcal per serving
- Total Fat: 10.8g
- Saturated Fat: 3.3g
- Net Carbohydrates: 5g
- Sugar: 1.5g

- Fiber: 0.6g
- Protein: 11.5g
- Sodium: 209.2mg
- Cholesterol: 10mg

 Cook time
0 minutes

 Prep. time
10 minutes

 Servings
4

Cooking Steps

1. Prepare you scallions by roughly slicing them, along with your fresh herbs. Add them into a food processor, along with the garlic, tahini and lemon juice.

2. Blitz until the mixture is as smooth as possible.

5. Spoon in the Greek yogurt and blitz until well mixed.

Greek Salad Dressing

We love this tangy, balanced dressing over your favorite fresh greens, Greek salad or over grilled chicken!

Ingredients

- 1 Garlic Clove, minced
- ½ cup Extra-Virgin Olive Oil
- 1tbsp Tahini
- 3tbsp Sherry Vinegar
- 1tbsp Lemon Juice
- 1tsp Dijon mustard
- 1tsp dried Oregano
- 1tsp dried Basil
- 1tsp Sumac
- Flaky salt
- Ground Black Pepper

Nutrition Values

- 132 kcal per serving
- Total Fat: 14.8g
- Saturated Fat: 2.1g
- Net Carbohydrates: 0.4g
- Sugar: 0g
- Fiber: 0g
- Protein: 0.3g
- Sodium: 15.7mg
- Cholesterol: 0mg

 Cook time
0 minutes

 Prep. time
10 minutes

 Servings
4-8

Cooking Steps

1. In a food processor, combine the garlic, vinegar, lemon juice, mustard, oregano, basil, sumac and seasoning.

2. Blitz until the mixture is smooth and add the tahini and pulse.

3. In a slow stream pour in the olive oil and continue to blend until emulsified and smooth.

4. Keep in the fridge until ready to serve. Don't worry if it splits, just be sure to shake the bottle before pouring over.

Snacks & Desserts

- Vanilla Panna Cotta With An Orange Jelly

- Dark Chocolate Sumac Truffles

- Scones With Fig & Strawberry Sumac Jam

- Vegan Carrot Cake

- Caramel Sumac Popcorn

- Sesame Tahini Energy Balls

- Honeydew Melon With Yogurt & Pink Peppercorns

- Honey And Sumac Lavash Crackers With Whipped Goats Cheese Dip

- Mixed Berry Sumac Sorbet

Vanilla Panna cotta with an Orange Jelly

Vanilla and sumac go hand in hand - the sherbetty sumac cuts through the creamy vanilla perfectly. Try replacing half the cream with skimmed milk for a lower fat, lighter alternative.

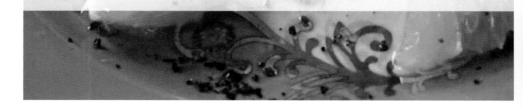

Ingredients

- 3.4 cups Double Cream
- 1 tbsp. Vanilla Bean Paste
- 0.1 cups Rum
- 5oz. (142g) Caster Sugar
- 3 Gelatine Leaves
- 2 Oranges

Nutrition Values

- 677 kcal per serving
- Total Fat: 61.8g
- Saturated Fat: 38.6g
- Net Carbohydrates: 25.6g
- Sugar: 25.6g
- Fiber: 0g
- Protein: 2g
- Sodium: 26mg
- Cholesterol: 0mg

 Cook time
Overnight

 Prep. time
20 minutes

 Servings
6

Cooking Steps

1. Put 1 gelatine leave in a bowl of cold water and allow for it to bloom whilst prepping the jelly.

2. Zest both oranges and set aside. Then juice both oranges into a saucepan.

3. Put the saucepan on a high heat and warm the orange juice to a simmer.

4. Immediately add the gelatine leave, after squeezing it dry using your hands and whisk the mixture.

5. Once the gelatine is fully melted and interspersed, fill each panna cotta mould with about an inch of the jelly liquid.

6. Put in the fridge and allow to set for an hour.

7. Meanwhile, make the panna cotta by putting the cream, vanilla, rum and sugar into a large saucepan on a medium-low heat.

8. Add the other two gelatine leaves into the cold-water bowl and allow them to bloom too.

9. Slowly heat up the mixture, stirring all the while, until the milk is just about to simmer. Do not allow it to reach boiling point.

10. Turn off the heat and whisk through the gelatine leaves. Allow the mixture to cool to warm.

11. Take the panna cotta moulds out of the fridge and pour the mixture up until just beneath the top.

12. Put back in the fridge and allow for the panna cottas to set overnight, or during the day.

13. When turning them out, dip them quickly in and out of a bowl of boiling hot water. This will just melt the edges, so the panna cotta and jelly come out with ease.

14. Top liberally with a sprinkle of sumac, which is sherbet-like in character on this dish, making it delightful.

Dark Chocolate Sumac Truffles

These dairy free and gluten free dark chocolate truffles are devilishly smooth and moreish. We love the sherbet sensation that the sumac delivers. Be daring and try these with chilli powder too.

Ingredients

- 7oz. (198g) 70 % Dark Chocolate
- 1.4oz. (40g) Caster Sugar
- ½ cup Water
- 1.5 tbsp. Chai Loose Tea
- 1 Peppermint Tea Bag
- ½ tbsp. of Sumac

Nutrition Values

- 212 kcal per truffle
- Total Fat: 10.9g
- Saturated Fat: 0g
- Net Carbohydrates: 26g
- Sugar: 20.8g
- Fiber: 0g
- Protein: 2.3g
- Sodium: 0mg
- Cholesterol: 0mg

 Cook time
10 minutes

 Prep. time
75 minutes

 Servings
4-6

Cooking Steps

1. Bring the tea, water, sugar and sumac to the boil and then allow it to simmer for 3 minutes.

2. Let the mixture completely cool and pass through a fine sieve. Return to the heat and allow it to simmer.

3. In a large, heat-proof bowl, break in the chocolate in small pieces. Pour the tea over the chocolate, whisking thoroughly until completed melted and thickened.

4. Try the ganache to see the strength of the flavor. Add a few drops of essence or essential oil, like cardamom, orange or spearmint.

5. Allow for the ganache to set for at least an hour in the fridge before taking out and shaping into balls quickly. Use a teaspoon to size the ganache and then roll into balls.

6. You can then roll them through cocoa powder or

7. dip them into melted tempered chocolate and allow them to drip dry. Sprinkle over some sumac and serve chilled.

Scones with Fig & Strawberry Sumac Jam

Another gorgeous homemade gift idea. These delectable scones will keep for between 3-4 days and the jam will keep for a whole month! Try the beautiful fig jam on toast or with a slice of rich chocolate cake.

Ingredients

- 16oz. (454g) Self-Rising Flour
- 2oz. (57g) Caster Sugar
- 3.5oz. (99g) Unsalted Butter, diced and chilled
- 2 Large Egg
- ⅕ cup Milk
- 2 tbsp. Yogurt
- 2 tsp. Baking Powder
- ½ tsp. Salt
- 6 Figs, quartered
- Juice of 1 Orange
- 6 Large Strawberries, chopped and halved
- 1 tbsp. Sumac
- ⅓ cup Caster Sugar
- ½ cup Water

Nutrition Values

- 511 kcal per serving
- Total Fat: 16.8g
- Saturated Fat: 9.4g
- Net Carbohydrates: 79.6g
- Sugar: 24.5g
- Fiber: 4.8g
- Protein: 11.2g
- Sodium: 27.8mg
- Cholesterol: 97.6mg

 Cook time
Overnight

 Prep. time
20 minutes

 Servings
6

Cooking Steps

1. Preheat the oven to 356 F and line a baking tray with parchment paper.

2. Sift the flour, sugar, salt and baking powder in a large bowl.

3. Scatter the cubed pieces of butter into the flour and begin to rub the two together, using your fingertips. This should become a crumbly mixture.

4. In a small bowl, whisk together the eggs with the milk and yogurt and stir into the flour mixture using a palette knife. It should form a soft dough. If there are many crumbs at the bottom, add a tablespoon more of milk to bring them together.

5. Form the dough into a bowl, working lightly and without needing it. The dough should look rough and shaggy, not perfect.

6. Tip the dough out onto a lightly floured surface and press it out until it's an inch thick.

7. Take a 6 cm round cutter, stamp it in flour and then stamp it in the dough, transferring the scones straight onto a tray. Be sure to set them apart slightly to give them space to expand a little. You can remold the dough to create scones out of your trimmings.

8. Place in the oven for about 12 minutes, or until golden brown on the top.

9. Meanwhile, make your jam.

10. Put the figs, strawberries, sugar, orange juice, sumac and water into a small saucepan and allow for it to come to the boil.

11. Boil the jam for about 10 minutes or until the figs are soft and disintegrated.

12. Once the jam has thickened nicely, pour it into a jam jar and allow for it to cool down before sealing it and transferring to the fridge.

13. Enjoy the warm jam topped on the fresh scones.

Vegan Carrot Cake

Our favorite vegan carrot cake is packed full of flavor and is surprisingly light. The milled chia seeds can be replaced with psyllium husk powder as a substitute but for best results this recipe is precise.

Ingredients

- ½ cup Vegetable Oil
- 6oz. (170g) Caster Sugar or Brown Sugar
- 2 tsp. Vanilla Extract
- 2 tbsp. Orange Juice or Zest
- cups Oat Milk
- 1 tsp. Apple Cider Vinegar
- 0.5oz. (14g) Milled Chia Seeds
- 11.5oz. (326g) Self-rising Flour
- tsp. Baking Powder
- 1 ½ tsp. Bicarbonate of Soda
- ½ tsp. Ground Cinnamon
- 1 tsp. Ground Nutmeg
- 1 tsp. Pumpkin Spice
- 2 tbsp. Sumac
- ½ tsp. Fine Sea Salt
- 3.5oz. (99g) Walnuts, chopped
- 11oz. (312g) Carrots, grated
- 2oz. (57g) Vegan Butter/ Margarine
- - 7oz. (141g) Violife Cream Cheese
- 1 tsp. Vanilla Extract
- 1lb 8oz. (227g) Icing Sugar, sifted

Nutrition Values

- 887 kcal per serving
- Total Fat: 30.5g
- Saturated Fat: 5.5g
- Net Carbohydrates: 147.4g
- Sugar: 111.7g
- Fiber: 3.7g
- Protein: 8.6g
- Sodium: 204.1mg
- Cholesterol: 10.6mg

 Cook time
40 minutes

 Prep. time
30 minutes

 Servings
4

Cooking Steps

1. Preheat the oven to 356 F. Line two 7" cake tins with parchment paper.

2. In a free-standing mixer, whisk together oil, sugar, vanilla and orange until the sugar is almost dissolved.

3. In a measuring jug, whisk together the milk and the apple cider vinegar (if it thickens or splits this doesn't matter).

4. Add the milled chia seeds to the oil and sugar mixture and whisk again for 30 seconds. Just until the mixture comes together.

5. In a slow stream, pour in the milk and vinegar mixture, still whisking until just combined.

6. In a separate bowl, sift together the flour, baking powder, cinnamon, bicarbonate, nutmeg, mixed spice, salt and sumac.

7. Stir this together and shake it into the wet mixture. Whisk until it's mixed in properly.

8. Add the grated carrots and chopped walnuts, fold until combined and divide the batter between the prepared cake tins.

9. Bake in the oven for 25 minutes and allow the cakes to cool for 10 minutes before tipping them out of their tins. Tip one of them onto a plate upside, which will leave a nice flat surface for the bottom tier. Put the other sponge on a cooling rack, the right way up.

10. When the cakes have cooled, make the frosting using an electric whisk.

11. Beat together the vegan butter and cream cheese until fluffy, then add the vanilla.

12. Sift the icing sugar into the bowl and whisk until the frosting is smooth and whipped.

13. If the icing isn't thick enough, you can always add more sifted icing sugar.

14. Put the flat cake on a plate and dollop the frosting on the first layer. Spread with a pallet knife, leaving an inch of the edge so that when the next layer is put on top, the frosting doesn't overflow.

15. Position the next sponge on top and dollop the rest of the icing on top, using the pallet knife again to smooth it out. This time go right to the edges.

16. Finish the cake with a sprinkle of sumac round the edges and some halved walnuts.

Caramel Sumac Popcorn

Play with different flavor combinations like adding desiccated coconut & chocolate powder or chili powder & sesame seeds to the popcorn. Or, simply dust with sumac for a lower calorie snack!

Ingredients

- 3tbsp Coconut Oil
- ½ cup of Popcorn Kernels
- 1/2tsp Salt
- 1 cup Golden Caster Sugar

- ¾ cup of Salted Butter
- 1tsp Vanilla
- 1tsp Sumac

Nutrition Values

- 154 kcal per serving
- Total Fat: 10.8g
- Saturated Fat: 3.3g
- Net Carbohydrates: 5g
- Sugar: 1.5g

- Fiber: 0.6g
- Protein: 11.5g
- Sodium: 209.2mg
- Cholesterol: 10mg

Cook time
10 minutes

Prep. time
10 minutes

Servings
4

Cooking Steps

1. In a large skillet with a lid, heat your oil until its completely melted.

2. Swirl the oil around the pan and sprinkle in the salt and then the kernels.

3. Toss and shake the kernels around the pan to coat them in oil.

4. Put the pan on a medium-low heat and place the lid on. Allow the corn to cook until it's all finished popping. You know it's finished when the popping noises have gone.

5. Once the corn is done, put it in the biggest bowl you have and turn off the heat.

6. In a saucepan, cube your butter into the bottom and put on a low heat. Then sprinkle over the sugar, vanilla and sumac, stirring until the sugar is dissolved.

7. Increase the heat to a medium-high and boil the mixture for 4-5 minutes. It should change from grainy to a smooth thick caramel. Be aware that the caramel can turn too dark at any second, so towards the end, swirl the caramel in the pan and be sure to keep an eye out for that perfect golden colour.

8. Immediately, pour the caramel into the bowl of popcorn and fold it with a spatula. Keep folding and mixing the caramel until the popcorn is almost evenly coated.

9. Pour the popcorn onto a baking tray, patting it out with the spatula, so that it's spread across the entirety of the tray. This will ensure the popcorn cools nicely without it sticking together in one big clump.

10. You can tap and crack the popcorn with a wooden spoon to break it up and get rid of any clumps.

11. Allow to cool and then munch munch munch. You can sprinkle and extra bit of sumac over the popcorn if you like that sherbet flavour.

Sesame Tahini Energy Balls

These bliss balls make the perfect gift for that vegan friend! Once they have chilled and set, place them in a cute box and tie with a lovely bow. You can even dust these with organic cocoa powder for extra sweetness.

Ingredients

- 16 Pitted Medjool Dates
- 1oz. (28.3g) Pumpkin or Sunflower Seeds
- 1oz. (28.3g) Hazelnuts, chopped
- ½ oz. (14g). Milled Chia Seeds

- 2 tsps. Vanilla Powder
- 2 tsps. Sumac
- 2 tbsp. Tahini
- 4 tbsp. Sesame Seeds
- Pinch of Flaky Sea Salt

Nutrition Values

- 103 kcal per serving
- Total Fat: 7.9g
- Saturated Fat: 0.9g
- Net Carbohydrates: 7.6g
- Sugar: 0.1g

- Fiber: 1.4g
- Protein: 4.9g
- Sodium: 0.8mg
- Cholesterol: 0mg

 Cook time
10 minutes

 Prep. time
60 minutes

 Servings
6

Cooking Steps

1. Pit the dates and add them to the food processor, followed by the seeds, hazelnuts, milled chia seeds, vanilla, sumac, tahini and salt.

2. Blitz everything in the food processor until it becomes a stick dough. You can make it as smooth as you like, depending on the power of your processor. You can also take out half the mixture and blitz the dough in batches to make it extra smooth.

3. Roll out the mixture into tablespoon sized balls and then roll them through a bowl of the sesame seeds until coated.

4. Put the balls in the refrigerator for an hour in an airtight container to ensure they set before eating.

Honeydew Melon with Yogurt & Pink Peppercorns

You wouldn't have thought it but melon, plus yogurt, plus pink peppercorns and sumac is a great combination. The honey sweet melon and spices are sensational and will boost any dull day!

Ingredients

- Half a small Honeydew Melon
- 2 tbsp Coconut Yogurt
- 1 tbsp crushed Pink Peppercorns
- Drizzle of Manuka Honey
- 1 tbsp Sumac

Nutrition Values

- 40 kcal per serving
- Total Fat: 0.4g
- Saturated Fat: 0.2g
- Net Carbohydrates: 8.9g
- Sugar: 8.2g
- Fiber: 0.4g
- Protein: 0.6g
- Sodium: 10.4mg
- Cholesterol: 0.9mg

 Cook time
0 minutes

 Prep. time
10 minutes

 Servings
6

Cooking Steps

1. Slice your melon in half lengthways.

2. Slice your melon in half again length ways and cut two of the halves into four slices of melon.

3. Using only half the melon, you should have 8 slices.

4. Put the slices on a platter and drizzle the melon with manuka honey.

5. Dollop the yogurt on, making sure each melon is covered and finish by sprinkling with the peppercorns and sumac.

Honey and Sumac Lavash Crackers with Whipped Goats Cheese Dip

These homemade crackers are tastier and healthier than store-bought, with no additives, and are the perfect accompaniment to this luscious whipped dip or your next cheese board! Brush with honey right before serving to keep them crisp.

Ingredients

- ½ cup of Lukewarm water
- 1 ½ tsp. active dry Yeast
- 1 cup Whole meal Bread Flour
- 1 cup All-purpose Flour
- 1 tbsp. Honey
- 2 tbsp. Extra-Virgin Olive Oil
- 1 tsp. Sea Salt
- 1 Egg White

- 1 tbsp. Sumac
- 1 tbsp. Honey
- 1 tbsp. Sesame Seeds
- 3.5oz. (99.2g) Goats Cheese
- 3.5oz. (99.2g) Cream Cheese
- 1 tbsp. Extra Virgin Olive Oil
- A pinch of sea salt

Nutrition Values

- 497 kcal per serving
- Total Fat: 32.1g
- Saturated Fat: 14.4g
- Net Carbohydrates: 36.5g
- Sugar: 8.3g

- Fiber: 3.5g
- Protein: 15.3g
- Sodium: 95.8mg
- Cholesterol: 28.5mg

 Cook time
30 minutes

 Prep. time
90 minutes

Servings
4-8

Cooking Steps

1. In a stand mixer with a dough hook, put the yeast and warm water and mix well. Allow to stand for 10 minutes.

2. Add the flours, oil, honey and salt and knead the dough for 10 minutes on a medium-low speed. Take out the formed dough and add a little extra virgin olive oil into the bottom of the bowl. Put the dough back in, cover with plastic wrap and let it prove for 30 minutes, in a warm place.

3. Divide the dough into 2 equal portions, cover with the plastic and let it rise for another 20 minutes.

4. Coat one side of a baking sheet with oil and lay on a flat tray.

5. Roll out the dough on a lightly floured surface. Keep the rest covered to make sure it doesn't dry out. Roll the dough into an 18" x 12" rectangle.

6. Place it on the prepared tray and roll it out to the edges.

7. Brush lightly with the egg white and put the first tray in for 12-15 minutes or until lightly browned and crispy.

8. Brush lightly with the egg white and put the first tray in for 12-15 minutes or until lightly browned and crispy.

9. Leave to cool on a wire rack and roll out the other dough balls, repeating the process.

10. Heat the other tablespoon of honey in a saucepan and once melted and runny, brush onto the crackers using a pastry brush.

11. Sprinkle over the sumac, a touch of extra sea salt and the sesame seeds. Store them in an airtight container or wrap in Clingfilm until needed.

12. To make the whipped goats' cheese, place the goats' cheese, cream cheese, olive oil and sea salt into a food processor. Ensure that all the casing is cut off of the goats' cheese before adding it, otherwise the dip will be lumpy. Blend until it's completely smooth and whipped. Season with a little sumac and crushed black pepper.

Mixed Berry
Sumac Sorbet

This refreshing berry sorbet can also be used for a morning smoothie bowl. Simply add granola, acai powder or chia and sliced ripe banana to make this into a meal.

Ingredients

- 3 cups of Mixed Berries, frozen
- 1tbsp Lemon Juice, freshly squeezed
- 2tbsp Sumac

- 1 egg white
- 2tbsp Orange Juice or Orange Liqueur
- 2 tbsp Runny Honey

Nutrition Values

- 92 kcal per serving
- Total Fat: 0.4g
- Saturated Fat: 0g
- Net Carbohydrates: 22.3g
- Sugar: 17.6g

- Fiber: 2.3g
- Protein: 1.7g
- Sodium: 25.4mg
- Cholesterol: 0mg

 Cook time
0 minutes

 Prep. time
Overnight

 Servings
4

Cooking Steps

1. Place the fruit, sumac and juices into a large food processor or blender and blitz until smooth.

2. Whisk the egg white into soft peaks and fold through the mix, if using at this stage.

3. Ensure the mixture is homogenous and then transfer into a small container.

4. Chill in the freezer overnight or for 3-4 hours at least.

5. Garnish with fresh aromatic mint sprigs and a few berries.

Beverages

1. Botanical Sumacade

2. Blueberry, Mint And Sumac Tea

3. Orange Sumac Energy Shot

Botanical Sumacade

We love these eye-widening sumac lemonades, which pop in your mouth as you drink them. Sumac syrup is fabulously diverse and can also be used when making cocktails, coating cake sponges or glazing sweet sticky pork.

Ingredients

- 2 cup Water
- 2 cup Sugar
- 3tbsp Sumac

- 4 cups Lemon or Plain Soda
- 1tbsp Lemon Juice
- 4tbsp Pink Peppercorns, crushed

Nutrition Values

- 387 kcal per serving
- Total Fat: 0g
- Saturated Fat: 0g
- Net Carbohydrates: 100g
- Sugar: 99.8g

- Fiber: 0g
- Protein: 0g
- Sodium: 1mg
- Cholesterol: 0mg

Cook time
5 minutes

Prep. time
10 minutes

Servings
4

Cooking Steps

1. Put the water and sugar into a small saucepan over a medium heat and whisk to completely dissolve sugar.

2. Allow the syrup to come to boil, turn off the heat and add the sumac.

3. Let the sumac infuse whilst the syrup cools down. Then strain the mixture using a fine mesh sieve.

4. Fill a glass of choice with the ice cubes and fill with the soda water and lemon juice.

5. Stir in the sumac syrup and sprinkle with the crushed pink peppercorns.

6. Serve as an aperitif or cooler on a warm winters evening. You can even add gin and replace the soda with tonic to make this a Sumac G&T.

Blueberry, Mint and Sumac Tea

Our favorite herbal tea for an added spring to your step during the day or a freshen up for the evening. Using the blueberries is optional but we love that it adds extra essential vitamins to the tea, such as folate and manganese.

Ingredients

- 4 cups Water
- 3 Green Tea Bags
- 2tbsps Sumac

- ½ cup of Blueberries
- 1tbsp Lemon Juice
- 1tbsp Honey

Nutrition Values

- 41 kcal per serving
- Total Fat: 0.1g
- Saturated Fat: 0g
- Net Carbohydrates: 9.9g
- Sugar: 8.8g

- Fiber: 0.4g
- Protein: 0.1g
- Sodium: 0.2mg
- Cholesterol: 0mg

 Cook time
0 minutes

 Prep. time
10 minutes

 Servings
4

Cooking Steps

1. Bring the water to a simmer in a large saucepan.

2. Add the blueberries, honey, lemon and sumac and bring to the boil or until the blueberries start to disintegrate.

3. Turn off the heat and add the tea bags. Allow them to infuse for 4 minutes, then take them out.

4. Strain the tea using a sieve strainer. Be sure to push out all the juices using a spatula.

5. Serve in a glass with a few sprigs of mint.

Orange Sumac Energy Shot

Be sure to get your digestive system going in the morning with one of these fiery shots. The punchy flavors make them a great pre-breakfast drink to consume a tricky but essential wellness add-in like spirulina powder!

Ingredients

- Juice of 2 Oranges
- Juice of 1 Lemon
- 4cm of Fresh Ginger, peeled and grated
- 2tsp Sumac

- 2tsp Turmeric
- 2tsp Cayenne Pepper
- A pinch of Black Pepper
- 1tbsp Manuka Honey

Nutrition Values

- 41 kcal per serving
- Total Fat: 0.1g
- Saturated Fat: 0g
- Net Carbohydrates: 11.2g
- Sugar: 9.2g

- Fiber: 0.3g
- Protein: 0.6g
- Sodium: 0.3mg
- Cholesterol: 0mg

 Cook time
0 minutes

 Prep. time
5 minutes

 Servings
4

Cooking Steps

1. Juice your oranges and lemon into a medium bowl.

2. Grate into the bowl the ginger and sprinkle in the sumac, turmeric and cayenne pepper.

3. Mix with a spoon and add the honey, continuing to stir until completely combined.

4. Sprinkle in the black pepper and serve the drink immediately into four large shot glasses.

We hope you enjoyed our recipes and were inspired to include the superfood spice, sumac in more of your meals!

As you may know, people like you depend on reviews to make sure they are buying the best books that suit their needs.

Every review is important to us, we take time to read them and we can make improvements when our valued customers suggest them.

We would greatly appreciate it if you could take a few minutes out of your day and leave us a review.

Printed in Great Britain
by Amazon